"IT'S OKAY,

YOU'RE WITH MY FATHER"

God bless!

Chris Shelton

"IT'S OKAY,

YOU'RE WITH MY FATHER"

(A CHILD ABUSE INVESTIGATOR'S CALL TO THE CHURCH)

WILLIAM "CHRIS" SHELTON

WESTBOW
PRESS
A DIVISION OF THOMAS NELSON

Notice: This book deals with cases of child abuse, restoration, and breaking cycles of abuse. The author believes it to be an important message to The Church; however, it may be extremely difficult for some readers. This book should be read prayerfully.

WestBow Press books may be ordered through booksellers or by contacting:

WestBow Press
A Division of Thomas Nelson
1663 Liberty Drive
Bloomington, IN 47403
www.westbowpress.com
1-(866) 928-1240

Because of the dynamic nature of the Internet, any web addresses or links contained in this book may have changed since publication and may no longer be valid. The views expressed in this work are solely those of the author and do not necessarily reflect the views of the publisher, and the publisher hereby disclaims any responsibility for them.

Certain stock imagery © Thinkstock.
Any people depicted in stock imagery provided by Thinkstock are models, and such images are being used for illustrative purposes only.

ISBN: 978-1-4497-2079-7 (e)
ISBN: 978-1-4497-2078-0 (sc)

Library of Congress Control Number: 2011932804

Printed in the United States of America

WestBow Press rev. date: 9/23/2011

FOREWORD & ENDORSEMENTS

"Chris Shelton is a man on a mission and with a message. His book "It's Okay, You're With My Father" (A Child Abuse Investigator's call to the Church) is a must read and one that all should take seriously. Sadly in society (and church circles) too often the thing we need to talk about the most we discuss the least. Chris is a former Special Agent and also a senior pastor and both roles have allowed him to expose the darkness of sin that has robbed millions of children of their innocent, formative years. Like a seasoned agent he extracts the negative and points people towards the positive with compassion and restoration. I cannot think of anyone with the author's expertise on this subject and I encourage all educators, civic leaders, business leaders, parents and concerned citizens to glean from this insightful book. The book in your hand will bring hope to the hurting and timely answers to those with questions. Lives hang daily in the balance and this book will help folks both survive and thrive and help rescue countless victims from throwing in the towel. It is a must read! Read this book and save a life. Don't delay, grab your copy today."

Frank Shelton
Evangelist & former Capitol Hill staff
Author, "Final Approach" (Career vs. Calling)
Waldorf MD, www.FrankShelton.com

"William "Chris" Shelton is counted among my closest friends. He has been my prayer partner for several years. As the County Administrator for the Arkansas Department of Human Services in Clay County, I have knowledge of Chris' abilities as a child abuse investigator. As a minister of Paragould Christian Church, I have knowledge of Chris' academic knowledge of the Bible. As a prayer partner and friend, I have knowledge of Chris' love and devotion to Jesus and his desire to see the Kingdom grow. I highly recommend the reading of his book."

Duane Dutka
Clay County DHS Administrator
Senior Minister, Paragould Christian Church
(www.ParagouldChristian.com)
Missionary to Ukraine orphanages

"I have known Chris Shelton for several years and have worked several cases together that were successful because of his ability and dedication. Chris is guided by his belief in God and a desire to do the right thing for the right reason. He is a person who will influence many people in the future for the betterment of all."

Glenn E. Leach
Chief of Police, Rector, AR

---

*"I like to write stories people want to read. Chris Shelton has written a work people **need** to read."*

Roland Mann
Author, "Buying Time"
www.rolandmann.wordpress.com

"As a sixteen year veteran of law enforcement I was amazed at this book. This book is a must read for everyone. Chris has a job that very few in law enforcement can do or will do. He is a true professional and a master at his craft as evident in his book. The book will restore one's faith in the belief that there is someone above who is watching over us all. When I had the pleasure to read the rough draft, I told Chris this book would be published. Now I can't wait to see the final version."

Shane Martin

"I believe Chris Shelton's writing will inspire many to do more and help people more. I have known Chris, his wife Jackie and their son, Adam for more than seven years. They are a reflection of what a Christian family should be. He has related his experiences with law enforcement and families in crisis in such a way that allows hope to rise for the restoration of wounded lives. He has been a pastor and ordained minister for years with Christian Family Fellowship International Inc. As president and senior elder of our fellowship I can say how proud I am of this man and his accomplishments. He is on the front lines reaching out to hurting families helping them to find a way to recovery."

Kevin D. McAnulty
Senior Pastor
Christian Family Fellowship International, Poplar Bluff, MO

"Chris Shelton has spent a lifetime working, studying, and devoting his life to being a better person and mentor to men. Everyone who meets Chris has become a better person from knowing him. Working in child protective services, he was an asset to law enforcement and a friend to children and their families. His work ethic and heart for helping children and their families is a bonus for DHS. Through his life experience and listening to God's Voice, Chris is a friend for children, parents, and the family as whole. His work ethic and devotion to his family is an example for everyone to follow. I am extremely pleased that he took the time to put his experiences and life wisdom down in book that will impact us all."

David Mote
Greene County DHS Administrator
Pastor, Providence Baptist Church at Gum Point Arkansas
Prayer partner with Chris Shelton

———————————————

"As a law enforcement officer with 17 years experience and a professional working in the area of Child abuse investigations, I have developed great faith in Chris both as a person and as a professional. I believe the information in this book will enlighten readers to challenges facing our society in this day and age that need to be brought out into the open. I believe it also provides encouragement while bringing attention to these challenges."

Rhonda R. Thomas

"The book ,"Its ok, You Are with My Father" (A Child Abuse Investigator's call to the Church) by Chris Shelton, is the inside story of one who has been there, one who has worked with victims, but one who still had the love of Christ in him when dealing with perpetrators. There was never a task too small or too large for Chris to tackle if it helped to find justice for victims or their families. Chris stood for the children and often the terms of justice were creative, sometime amazing, but always filled with his prayers. While reading the book, I could visualize the characters and could see Chris giving support, but never losing sight of the importance of his belief that we are all children of god. I always felt during an investigation that Chris Shelton "had my back". He took small pieces of evidence and worked with each piece until the justice system had the whole. I am honored to recommend this book, it is written by a man who has been in the trenches, but did not forget what was important."

Cathy L Young, DNSc, FNP-BC
Coordinator of the Family Nurse Practitioner Track
Arkansas State University
College of Nursing and Health Professions
Jonesboro AR 72467

INTRODUCTION

"It's okay, you're with my father"... I had been taking my son and one of his friends home from a church youth group when they spotted a couple of troubled teenagers out on a lawn and immediately wanted me to pull over. It was a cold night, but neither of the teens was wearing jackets. They were both dressed "Goth" (unkempt, dark clothes, black fingernail polish), were known to use drugs and suspected of dabbling in the occult, but my son and his friend had been witnessing to the boys at school and had previously given them some Christian tracts. They had been drawn to the genuine but, regrettably, unusual concern for them, and approached the car. The taller of the two boys, and apparent leader, leaned in the front window and told me, "I don't normally care much for Christians, but these guys are different". I told them that they were probably the first real Christians he had ever met then. We had only just been there when a police car pulled up and one of the boys said, "Oh great, the cops hate me", but my son quickly and confidently replied, "Its okay, you're with my father"... I worked in child protective services for the state and was known by all the local law enforcement officers, but I was touched by my son's confidence and immediately thought, "shouldn't we all be just like that with our Heavenly Father?"

We had only just been there when a police car pulled up and one of the boys said, "Oh great, the cops hate me", but my son quickly and confidently replied, "Its okay, you're with my father". I worked in child protective services for the state and was known by all the local law enforcement officers, but I was touched by my son's confidence and immediately thought shouldn't we all be just like that with our Heavenly Father?

Unfortunately, we have an entire generation of kids out there who are being raised without fathers. The police had been called to the house on a domestic disturbance. One of the teenagers' father (who they sadly described as "the sperm donor") had shown up and gotten into an argument with the boy's mother. The "argument" had been bad enough that the neighbors had called the police. I stayed to support the police officer just in case things got out of hand. The father, though belligerent with the officer, left without incident. I was further touched when one of the teens looked at me and said, "One day I'd like to help people like you, too".

I actually knew my son had been witnessing to this boy at school due to a phone call from a well-intentioned teacher, who expressed how highly she thought of my son, but was concerned "with who he was hanging out with". I remember smiling when I realized where the conversation was going. I asked if my son had been doing anything wrong while with this young man and was told no. I then asked if the young man was doing anything wrong while with my son and was again told no. I thanked the teacher for her concern and asked that she call me if she ever saw them doing anything wrong while my son was with this young man, but I assured her that if my son was hanging around with this person, he was probably telling him about Jesus! The teacher had been well meaning and, had actually gone the extra mile to call me, so I was appreciative, but I also thought that it was sad that she didn't see past the troubled teen's exterior and realize the dysfunctional home in which he was trying to survive, let alone thrive. Sadly, I also looked around the neighborhood and wondered how many Christian families lived there who could have reached out to this family.

ABOUT THE AUTHOR

William "Chris" Shelton joined the Army out of high school becoming an infantry squad leader and using his G.I. benefits to complete a degree in Sociology with concentration in Education with aspiration of becoming a teacher, but was sidetracked when recruited to be a U.S. Army Counterintelligence Special Agent out of the Washington, DC area where he served another 5 years and was awarded a Meritorious Service Medal. He didn't feel he could personally be the husband and father he wanted to be traveling 30,000 flight miles a year, so he resigned. He is married to Jackie and the father of a teenage son (Adam). As of this writing, Chris is completing his eighth year as an investigator in child protective services and has recently completed ministry school. God has given him a vision for "Reach Out Christ's Kingdom" (ROCK) Ministries, reaching out and also encouraging other churches to reach out to families and individuals from difficult backgrounds; not attempting to "fix" them, but to provide an atmosphere of love, acceptance, and forgiveness where God can "heal" them. Also, working in child protective services, Chris has sadly observed a critical shortage of foster homes, which has also led him to encourage churches to prayerfully support foster parents from their congregation just as they would any missionary. Chris believes it is the only way we are going to break the cycles that are currently destroying our families.

WHY THIS BOOK

As a child abuse investigator, I've worked over a hundred cases a year for over eight years. It isn't that I live in a bad area. I live in "Bible belt America", an area with low crime and highly rated schools, but I've had the opportunity to deal with child caseworkers and investigators in other states and what I believe is due to the break down of traditional families, child abuse and neglect has become a National problem. I've spent countless hours in court waiting to testify, and with a heart concerned for these families I've prayed and asked God... what can we do? A State Representative who knew my work even asked me, "Chris, what can I do as a State Representative to help?" The truth is that the State can treat the symptoms, but only God can heal the problem. Social Service is traditionally the largest line item on all state budgets. I believe this is also due to the break down of traditional families. We have generations being raised without fathers in the homes. They are instead being raised by television shows like "Jerry Springer", "MTV Spring Break", and "Girls Gone Wild" ads. I try to start each day with a good Christian television program while I'm preparing for work, but just a few channels up is "Jerry Springer" with every kind of dysfunctional situation imaginable being exalted. Without some guidance, the average student is watching the "Jerry Springer" program getting ready for school in the morning. After school it is "MTV Spring Break" and just a little later a "Girls Gone Wild" ad which is virtually soft core pornography bordering on child pornography as it appears most of the girls are barely legal aged college students who appear almost inebriated on spring break being encouraged to act out sexually on camera. Just an additional note about these programs… I spent a year working with developmentally delayed young adults in State care. Left to their own they would invariably be watching trash like this and there would be problems in their group home getting along with each other. With a little encouragement to watch better programs there would be a much better living atmosphere in the homes. Is there any wonder why I've had to work cases involving a 14-year-old raping a 9-year-old or a 21-year-old raping a 14-year-old? Please know that I'm not picking on single mothers. They are, I believe for the most part, trying their best. I'm actually not picking on the men either. They weren't raised by a Godly father either. I guess I am looking at the Church. Not all churches of course; there are some (and more on the way thank God), that have already opened their doors and are reaching out to some of these young people and families. I'm aware of one church that has an after school program and another that held a young ladies purity conference which had a remarkable turn out for a small town. I'm aware of another that sponsored a "Power Team" group and over a hundred young people were led to the Lord. Unfortunately, I'm also aware of churches that have "uninvited" certain young people to not come back. May God forgive them for they know not what they do. Anyway, while waiting to testify in court and praying, God put it on my heart that the answer was Jesus, but how do we get Jesus into these families? Sadly, many of these families have been kicked so many times they are just waiting for the next boot. Especially sad is that in some cases it was immature Christians wearing the boots. We can't come at these families with a holier-than-thou attitude trying to "fix" them. They can spot another person condemning them a mile away, but are desperate for someone that will genuinely love them. We have to exercise God's love and provide an atmosphere of love, acceptance (not of the behavior, but of the person), and forgiveness where God can "heal" them. It is the only way that we can break the current cycles destroying families.

I'd like to ad an additional note about "Jerry Springer". Before I ever knew who "Jerry Springer" was, I once saw a legitimate journalistic piece he did which was very inspirational. I was shocked when I saw his current show and realized it was the same person. I'm sure he has made his fortune with his current show, but I pray and ask all who read this to stop a moment and pray for Jerry Springer. If he turned to God he could do a tremendous work in helping these young people that idolize him instead of encouraging them down paths that are destroying their lives. "MTV Spring Break" and "Girls Gone Wild" show young people drinking, partying, acting out sexually, and apparently having fun; however, what they don't show is the venereal diseases, the people who drank too much and died from alcohol poisoning or caused a car crash killing innocent victims, the unwanted pregnancies, the feelings afterward that lead to depression, low self esteem, etc. I remember a case where I had to respond to the emergency room, because a 17-year-old girl had been at a "party" where she shouldn't have been and was slipped drugs and used as a prostitute and dropped passed out outside the hospital emergency room. Numerous statistics from credible official sites show that 1 out of 4 sexually active teenagers is reported with a sexually transmitted disease each year; many without any visible symptoms and many incurable. Further statistics show 1 out of 4 girls being sexually molested before adulthood and 1 out of 6 boys. Isn't it time for The Church to rise up and reach out to these young people in love showing them the truth that God loves them and has a good plan for their lives. And that the lies being told them are to destroy their lives and to prevent them from experiencing the real joy that God has planned for them.

(There once was a man walking along the river and he saw a person drowning…)

There once was a man walking along the river and he saw a person drowning, so he did what anyone would and went in and pulled them to shore. But then he saw another and again he dove in. He then saw another and another and kept diving in till he was physically exhausted and could hardly move yet still again there were people drowning. All of a sudden another man came running along the shore and the first man called out, "Stop! Help me! People are drowning and I'm exhausted", but the second man called back, "Don't stop me. I'm going upstream to stop the person that is throwing them in!"

Nine years ago, I had the opportunity to go to work as a child abuse investigator for the state. It is something I have always done as a ministry and I believe I was able to be used by God to help a lot of children and families, but I've felt like the man that kept pulling drowning people out of the river one at a time till he was physically exhausted, but there was still people drowning. Now I feel God is using that experience and calling me to be the man that runs upstream to stop the person throwing them into the water. The person throwing them into the water is Satan.

A DISCLAIMER

I'm going to be writing about some of the cases I've worked, but it is my desire that this book not be about me. I also don't want this book to be just about a bunch of negative situations. It is my hope and prayer that when this book is read you'll forget about me and forget about the specific cases, but will remember to reach out in love so that God can use you to break the cycle and heal these families in Jesus.

As I begin to share some of the experiences I've had as an Investigator in Child Protective Services, I wanted to state that these cases are true and accurate to the best of my memory, but I will not disclose any identities of anyone involved. Any similarities to anyone should be considered a coincidence.

ACKNOWLEDGEMENTS

I want to stress that I didn't work these cases alone. I was one part of a team of good, professional (many Christian) men and women in local law enforcement agencies, nurses and doctors who performed the sexual abuse exams and had to take time away from their busy practices to testify in court, school teachers and counselors, prosecutors and children and family service attorneys who are over worked for state pay and could be making much more money practicing in other areas of law, and all the employees of Social Services who have dedicated their lives to families, also over worked for state pay, and to all the foster parents (God love you and we need so many more). You are all my heroes. I especially want to thank my wife and son. You were supportive of the call on my life to help kids. I could have been making more money and had more time at home for you, but you made the sacrifice also for the kids. When I first asked what you thought about me going into child protective services, I remember my son who was about 8-years-old at the time, he asked if that meant I'd have to work late and on weekends. When I told him that it would sometimes, but I'd be helping kids, he said, "It's okay then". I'm blessed to have a wife who has been so supportive. I haven't forgotten the times I was supposed to be taking you to dinner and instead had to run out on a case, or that every time I was woke up in the middle of the night to go out on a case that you were also, or how you stepped up at home while I was taking ministry school classes after work and working on this book. I'd also like to thank my parents who raised me without having to fear being abused and to protect those that can't protect themselves. You all share any credit for any good I've done, because I couldn't have done it alone. I also want to acknowledge all those who have survived being abused as children. God love you. Anytime I've been asked to speak at a college class or parent's group, I invariably have someone come up to me afterwards and tell how they have never discussed it before, but were abused while growing up. It was an attack by the devil, but I want to assure you that you can overcome and go on to help others. To those who have offended on children, God can forgive you and use you for good if you turn to him. If there is anyone out there who I failed to help, I'd like to share that I started each day with two prayers. The first was that I see all that I was supposed to see to help children. The second was that I also protect anyone from being wrongly accused. If anyone came up to me years later and asked if I remembered them and said I came to their house, but didn't help them, I needed to always be able to say that I always did my very best. Thank you also to all who have shared this vision and tolerated me while I was working it out in my head and putting it on paper. Thank you and God bless! I most especially and foremost want to thank Jesus Christ. Anything that I am or have accomplished is because of you. Thank you, Lord.

HOW DO YOU DEAL WITH CHILD ABUSERS WITHOUT HATING THEM

(The 14 page thank you letter from a man serving 25 years for molesting his daughter)

I routinely hear the comment, "Man, I don't know how you can deal with those people who abuse kids without wanting to hurt them... I couldn't do it." Well, personally I couldn't hurt someone else's kid let alone my own, but I was blessed to be raised by loving, Christian parents. I was never abused. We weren't rich, but I always had good clothes, a warm bed, and didn't have to worry if there would be food to eat. As a Christian, I look at each case as an opportunity to minister to a family. Also, when the caseload got especially heavy or I was dealing with an especially bad case, I could turn it over to God in prayer. I've seen Caseworkers who deal in child protective services who were good people, but not necessarily Christians (or mature Christians if they were), and the job would eat them up.

Dealing with over 100 cases a year for over 8 years I really only remember a very few offenders who had absolutely no remorse for their actions. These people had most likely been offended on themselves growing up to the point that they had become psychopaths. They had gotten to the point that they had to be locked away for the safety of society. If they get out, short of a miracle of God they'll offend on another child just as quickly as a situation to do so becomes available. I remember one of these who had molested a number of children before finally being caught. He said, "It happened to me when I was growing up and I survived, so there isn't any reason I shouldn't do it to as many kids as I can also."

I remember another case where a man was the most remorseful I had ever met. He had been molesting his own daughter. The mother had abandoned the child with the father (we've been seeing more of that). The little girl loved her father and wanted to protect him, but just wanted him to stop doing "that" to her, so she wasn't being very cooperative. Her father had been careful not to penetrate her so that there wouldn't be any physical evidence. There really wasn't going to be enough evidence for a prosecution without a confession. During the interview, God put it on my heart to ask the man to tell me about when he was abused. There had never been anything said before about this man being abused, but the question hit him like a ton of bricks. He looked at me and said, "I've never told anyone before about being abused growing up." "How did you know?" I encouraged him to go ahead and tell me. In tears, he broke down and told me that he had never before told anyone, but his mother had been a drug addict. He didn't know who is father was. As a small child his mother would lock him in a closet while she would go on a drug run. She locked him in the closet, because she didn't want the neighbors to see him alone in the house and call the police. Worse yet, she would go get her drugs, get high, and forget about her little boy locked in the closet. He described how he would lay down by the bottom of the door trying to get some fresh air and see light. How he would lose track of how long she was gone and how he would be afraid she wasn't coming back to let him out. He recalled when she did come home, she would pass out and her druggy friends would sexually molest him. He explained how he became addicted to pornography and sex at an early age. He stated

2

that he tried to control it and could for awhile, but then would break down. He confessed how his daughter had started to look like her mother and he would be tempted again. I'll never forget him telling me, "No one realizes the 999 times you were tempted and managed not to do it, but then you have a bad day, and no place to turn to for help, so you do it again." He was crying when he confessed to her telling him, "Please daddy, you said you wouldn't again". The man didn't want to go to prison, but he confessed, because he'd rather go to prison than see her pleading eyes as she once again had to say, "Please daddy, you said you wouldn't again". The man thanked me for treating him well even after what he had admitted doing. I told him that what he did was wrong, but I had never been abused like he had. It didn't excuse what he did, but who was I to judge him? When he was sent to prison, I sent a Bible and note with the chief jailor telling them his story, and that I believed him to be the most repentant man I'd ever met, and asked that they contact me if I could help. Soon after, I received a 14-page thank you letter. He was writing his life story and hoping that one day he could counsel other offenders. I hope and pray for his daughter and for him, that he stays that course.

THE CASE OF THE MAN WHO TRADED HIS STEP-DAUGHTER FOR DRUGS

(The power of listening to and obeying The Holy Spirit)

Over the years, I've been involved in 2 child death cases. They were more than tragic, but when I think of the worse case I've ever worked it had to be the one I'm about to share. The step-father of an 11-year-old girl was a drug addict. He had stopped with his step-daughter to make a drug purchase, but didn't have enough money and the dealer wouldn't give him credit; however, after seeing the step-daughter, the drug dealer volunteered to give the man drugs in exchange for letting him have sex with her. Perhaps it was what the step-father had in mind all along. He consented, went into another room to do his drugs while the drug dealer took the young girl into another bedroom and raped her. Her first sexual experience was being raped by a drug dealer at 11-years-old because step-daddy couldn't afford his drugs. Afterwards step-daddy was high and figured the drug dealer already had her, so he might as well also; threatening her with a large knife to keep her mouth shut. Worse, step-daddy liked it and after that would make her perform on him when she came home from school. The step-father also arranged a prescription for Ritalin (a drug prescribed for children with Attention Deficit Disorder) by lying to her doctor about her symptoms. She was required to take it at school, but the step-father showed her how to fake taking it at school, pocket it, and bring it back for him. He was shooting it up like heroin. I clearly remember, because I hadn't heard of it being abused like that before, but found out that although very dangerous, it was the latest thing for drug addicts. He additionally wouldn't "waste" his drug money on food or personal hygiene products for her, so she would never miss a day at school (breakfast, lunch, and step-daddy wanted that Ritalin). When she began her menstrual cycle, he told her to use rolled up toilet paper in place of feminine napkins. When school was out she became an expert of when people in the neighborhood would be eating and would make it a point to show up around that time.

The family moved from one county to the next before anyone became too suspicious and, sadly, she was 13 years old before a tip to the Child Abuse Hotline was assigned to me to investigate. The girl was understandably afraid to make a statement, but eventually did. I remember how matter-of-fact she was about the sexual abuse that occurred to her, but she was able to give a very detailed description of the drug dealer, what occurred, and the knife that her step-father had used to threaten her. She was taken into foster care and both her step-father and mother were arrested. The mother was arrested, because the girl confided in her mother, who refused to believe her and had thereby allowed the abuse to continue. During the investigation, the knife, and nude photography the step-father had taken of the girl were re-covered. When the stepfather was arrested and brought into the sheriff's office, his stench was so severe, that even though it was wintertime, the windows of the sheriff's vehicle had to be rolled down to bear the odor. His body odor was so bad when jailed that the prisoners were complaining and he had to be forced to shower. It was clear from the moment the stepfather was brought in that he hated our guts and wasn't going to cooperate. I actually sensed a demonic spirit over the man and believed his hatred was geared toward both me and the chief deputy because we were Christians. We had a detailed description of the drug dealer, but not his name, and we wanted to arrest both of them, but the stepfather refused to cooperate and made it clear that nobody else would either. We had enough evidence to prosecute the stepfather and put him away for a long time, but were at a standstill over identifying the drug dealer.

I prayed, asking what to do next and received one of the clearer instructions I've ever heard from The Holy Spirit. He told me to buy the stepfather a Bible. As you can tell from the previous chapter, I normally have a very Christian heart even to offenders, but this particular person had been so foul that even I was having a difficult time seeing him through God's eyes. But, wanting to be "obedient" to God, I purposed to buy him a cheap Bible. That quickly wasn't good enough for The Holy Spirit who added, "And not a cheap one!" When I got home I told my wife about what had happened and she initially said she didn't want us spending our hard earned money on this guy, but then quickly changed her heart and said we should do what The Holy Spirit said. I'd like to take a moment here and brag on my wife. She was adopted at birth and her adoptive mother had mental health problems and became an abusive alcoholic to her. She had a very difficult childhood herself. I consider her to be a miracle of God how she has grown into the lovely Christian woman she is today. Anyway, I went to the Christian book store and picked up a nice Bible to give to the stepfather. Now, because there was a pending prosecution, I was not permitted to give the Bible to the stepfather myself. He probably wouldn't have accepted it anyway, so I gave it to the chief jailer and asked that he give it to the stepfather, anonymously. About a month later I received a call from the jailer informing me that the stepfather wanted to see me. After arriving at the jail and meeting with the stepfather, I immediately noticed that the demonic spirit I'd sensed before was not there. The stepfather looked at me and said that someone had left a Bible at the jail for him... he then intently stared at me to see my reaction. I didn't tell him that it was me and, eventually, he said that he didn't have anything else to do while in jail and had finally broken down and started reading the Bible. He went on to say how he initially refused to read it, but would pick it up and throw it down, but then eventually started to read it. He said he was prepared to make a statement, in order for the drug dealer to be arrested also. I told him that I couldn't promise him any deals. He said he wasn't looking for any deals; that what he had done was wrong and he deserved to go to jail, but the drug dealer deserved the same. He gave us the information we needed for an arrest warrant to be put out for the drug dealer. Had I not been obedient to the Holy Spirit's prompting and bought him that Bible, we wouldn't have obtained the information we needed to arrest the drug dealer.

Now having an arrest warrant for the drug dealer and locating him to make the arrest are two entirely different things. The drug dealer knew that the little girl had been taken into foster care and that her stepfather had been arrested (funny how fast these things get around in that kind of community) and had taken off. I started interviewing anyone who might have a lead on where he was, but it was clear that everyone I spoke to was afraid of him. I kept hearing that I didn't know who I was dealing with and how bad he was or how dangerous. Now, I've been a U.S. Army infantry squad leader and a U.S. Army counterintelligence special agent. It takes quite a bit to make me nervous, but after hearing so many people who were genuinely afraid of this guy, I admit I was even beginning to get a little nervous about him. Finally, I got the call that he had been picked up. Arrangements were made for a polygraph examiner to do the interview. There was enough to prosecute this guy and put him away for quite awhile, but a confession is always cleaner in the event of an appeal and often leads to a plea agreement which prevents the victim from the trauma of having to testify, and also stops any appeal. It was clear when I saw him being brought in that he had been down this road before, had an attitude, and had no intention of cooperating. Suddenly, I had a very real sense that I needed to be in prayer about the interview. I also got on the phone to some serious Christians, and told them I needed them to be in prayer. After a while, the examiner left the drug dealer in the exam room and came to the adjacent room where I had been observing the interview through a monitor and speaker (and also keeping it in prayer). He said the guy wasn't cooperating, but asked if I wanted to come in and try since I'd been involved in the case from the beginning and might have an edge on the interview. I entered the room, introduced myself, and sat down, but hadn't had a chance to ask anything. He already knew who I was. It had gotten back to him that I was the one involved in the girl being taken into foster care. I felt the presence of The Holy Spirit heavy in the room and, all of sudden, the drug dealer began to break down and sob. I'll never forget his huge tears falling on the interview table so hard they bounced back up. He wasn't crying because he was afraid of me or even of going to prison. I believe he was crying under the conviction of The Holy Spirit over all the things he had done (and perhaps had been done to him as a child). He confessed to what had happened and, interestingly, his confession was virtually identical to the statement the girl had made, right down to the smallest details of what clothes she had been wearing. The stepfather and drug dealer both accepted a plea deal (I believe it was 25 years) and are in prison as of this writing. The girl's mother lost her parental rights for not protecting her daughter. And, thankfully, a Christian relative was given custody of the girl. I want to stress that this confession wasn't because of how "good" I was. I had hardly said anything. It was entirely the result of The Holy Spirit, and simply being open and obedient when hearing Him.

THE CASE OF THE VAMPIRE

**(My first experience with real spiritual
warfare and the power of prayer)**

People don't realize how the occult has infiltrated our society even in "Bible-belt America", but it has. I've seen a number of cases where the occult had been involved. One of the more disturbing cases I worked involved a man that had an occult alter in his home, had written on the walls in his own blood and had a pewter chalice from which he drank human blood. Witnesses said he liked to hang out in area cemeteries late at night. Witnesses further stated that he would cut himself and bleed into the chalice or use a syringe and draw blood out and put in the chalice to drink; that he had told women if he drank their blood that he owned their soul, and if they had a child together it would be a demon child. There was also testimony about orgies, drugs and pornography use.

One of the women he was seeing (she called herself his wife, but there was no record of a legal marriage) had a juvenile daughter from a previous marriage. One day while the mother was at work, he sexually fondled the daughter. The little girl reported telling her mother, but her mother accused her of lying. Thankfully, she then told a grandmother who took her directly to the sheriff's office and filed a report. The grandparents didn't know about their daughter's boyfriend's occult activities. Fortunately, the little girl hadn't been exposed to that part of her mother's boyfriend's activities yet either. The boyfriend was on parole for a previous crime and was brought in by his parole officer. It was clear during the interviews that the little girl was very credible and that the subject was lying, but he had been arrested before and wasn't going to confess. We were concerned that if the only thing standing between this man going back to jail for a long time was this little girl that she was in danger. Because he was already on parole, instead of a bail hearing, we requested a hearing to have his parole revoked, sending him back to prison pending the trial. Now, normally a parole revocation hearing is a pretty routine thing and usually doesn't last longer than around 20 minutes. This one, however, waged on for six hours! I was on the stand myself for around an hour-and-a-half, taking abuse from this man's attorney. Worse, the little girl was required to testify during the revocation hearing. None of us could believe what was going on! I've been in extended trials that weren't as intense. As a Christian though I recognized what was going on. This was a for real on the front lines spiritual battle being waged and we had went in unprepared... oh, we knew the case, but we had failed to take the time to pray before the hearing. The spiritual battle was so intense that you could feel the conflict overhead and very nearly even see it. It was like a shadowy darkness. It was the most physically and spiritually exhausting experience of my life. Thank God, after six hours we finally prevailed and the offender was sent back to prison pending his trial. Shortly after, the little girl's mother lost custody of her, because she tried to abscond her out-of-state so she couldn't testify against the boyfriend. She was overheard on jail visitation recordings stating she wasn't afraid of going to jail trying to protect her boyfriend from going back to prison. The boyfriend said he wasn't stupid and no one could make him change his story and that the whole case revolved around the little girl's testimony and she wouldn't be able to hold up in court.

As the time for the trial came around I had not forgotten that parole revocation hearing. It was the worst battle of my life and I wasn't looking forward to going back into it again. Also, during this time, someone had burned four black candles down facing north, south, east, & west, in the center of the cemetery adjacent to where I lived. I don't know if it was a coincidence or not, but it was next to a grave with the same last name as the boyfriend in this case. I suspect it wasn't a coincidence and that his coven was trying to cast spells. When it came time for the trial, I was determined this time to be ready. Not just with the case, but more importantly, spiritually. I contacted the Chief Deputy who was a very sincere Christian man. We went over to the court before the trial and prayed around the outside of the court. We prayed around the halls of the court and inside the court. We prayed for everyone we could possibly think of involved with the case including the offender and his attorney. When we couldn't possibly think of anything more to pray about, we took a break and went and got a cup of coffee before the trial began. When we came back to the court I could hardly believe the difference. The experience was like walking into the most wonderful church you could imagine. You could feel the presence of angels so strongly standing guard around the outside of the court building that you could almost see them. They were strong, standing tall, and it was like they were smiling… someone had finally put them to work. I could feel and almost see angels standing guard at all four corners of the court building and also standing guard on the corners of the court roof top. I could feel and almost see angels standing guard on each side of the outer doors leading into the court and also at the inner doors of the court. I could feel and almost see angels standing guard inside the court doors and at each of the four corners inside the court. I was facing one of the worst trials of my career, but felt more at peace than attending many churches. When it came time for me to be called as a witness I hadn't forgotten the grilling I'd taken by this same attorney at the parole hearing, but I was totally at peace. He approached the podium with the same zeal he had at the parole hearing and prepared to attempt to grill me just like he had before, but all of a sudden it was like something came over him. It was like he couldn't say anything bad. He finally just sat down again and I was excused. The little girl got on the stand and did a great job. I'll credit the attorney that he was a gentleman with the little girl and I later told him that if we ever faced each other in court again that I would only be remembering he had been appropriate with that little girl. After her testimony, the boyfriend leaned over and asked his attorney if he could still get a plea deal. He took a plea that gave up his right to an appeal. I had always believed in prayer, but for the first time I really got it.

THE DIVORCED WAITRESS

(The importance of a father)

In another case, a man had been sexually abusing his daughter. She finally told someone when she became afraid that he was starting to sexually abuse a younger sister also. The mother had been unaware of her husband sexually abusing their daughter. What I'll never forget though was her telling about his addiction to pornography. She told me in tears about the thousands and thousands of dollars this man had spent on pornography. She stated that he would try and stop and would get rid of it all, but then it would start creeping back into their home. He made a good living, but she stated how much the family could have used those thousands of dollars. I hate pornography because of what I've seen it do to families. Sadly, due to his arrest, the family was placed in a severe financial hardship as the mother had to sell their home and re-start their lives. I remembered thinking how it was the rape after the rape. Anyway, to continue with the story, there are two parts to a prosecution... the trial, and the sentencing phase after a person has been found guilty. At the sentencing phase, the jury is allowed to hear additional testimony that couldn't have been brought out in the trial such as prior convictions or character references when deciding the sentence. In this particular case, after the father had been found guilty in court, he was sitting there during the sentencing phase staring at his daughter... it wasn't a threatening stare, it wasn't a please forgive me stare; it was as if he was imagining being with her one last time as he knew he was going to be going to prison for a very long time. I remember that the judge was obviously very perturbed at the man and the jury was seething. I was expecting the judge to come down on him at any moment, but didn't. I guess a judge has to be careful to not allow any grounds for an appeal (which this person did and lost). There is a biker group called "Bikers Against Child Abuse" (B.A.C.A.). When a child has been abused, they volunteer to ride to court and escort the victim to prevent them from being afraid. We didn't have one of those groups, but I'm over six foot, 200 pounds and the Chief Deputy was a big man also. We got up and walked to in front of where the man was sitting and sat down directly in front of him... he turned back around.

At the sentencing phase I was asked to testify as to some of the effects of child sexual abuse on a daughter. I testified that a daughter develops her sense of self worth from a father and learns how men and women should relate in a healthy manner. I testified that it was common for girls that had been sexually abused to develop drug problems trying to deal with what happened (self medicating to make the inner pain go away), to either become sexually promiscuous (seeking love and confusing sex with love) or the opposite and become frigid with men. I continued that without really good counseling she could very likely end up having future relationship problems with men without even understanding why. An example was that she may have believed she'd overcome what happened and not be consciously thinking about it, but a future man might wear a certain aftershave, soap, or make a certain gesture that reminds her subconscious of what happened and she freezes up and pulls back emotionally without even knowing why. Without really good counseling she won't even understand what happened and the man won't understand either and it causes problems. I knew one young lady that developed "cutting" behaviors. It is where a person (often girls) "cut" themselves. I asked one young lady why she felt the compulsion to cut herself and I'll never forget her answer. She said it "let the pain out".

I shared this to tell you about a certain waitress. I had worked through lunch and finally got an opportunity to stop for something to eat. It was after the lunch rush and the restaurant had emptied out. The waitress saw me pray over my lunch before eating. Now I don't make a big deal out of praying over my food, but I do take a moment and discreetly thank God and acknowledge Him as Lord. The waitress knew what I did for a living, evidently needed someone to talk to, and felt comfortable after seeing me pray over my food. She told me how she had just been left by her third abusive relationship. I recognized that she had been abused in her past and offered to pray with her. She answered that she wasn't a Christian. I said I'd still be happy to pray for her and that what she was seeking was God. That He loved her and had a good plan for her life. I'll never forget her telling me that it was hard to trust after so many men had been abusive to her. Fortunately, I had a Christian tract I was able to leave with her. I later saw her again and she thanked me for sharing the tract. I could see there was a new inner happiness as she told me how she had shared the tract with several of the other waitresses.

THE CASE OF THE DARK ELF REALM

(The dark side of role playing games)

Unless I'd actually been doing this work, I don't think I would have believed how many 13 & 14-year-old girls I've interviewed that told me about their fifth, sixth, and seventh sexual partners since they were as young as 11-years-old. The youngest pregnancy I've dealt with was an 11-year-old that got pregnant in the back seat of a friend's borrowed car. She told me they only did it the one time, it wasn't at all how she thought it would be, she didn't enjoy it, and what I won't forget her telling me was how she was supposed to be on the cheerleading squad, but now she was getting ready to be a mother at 12-years-old. In many cases, the "boys" they were having sex with were anywhere from 15 to 24-years-old. I'm reminded of a particular 23-year-old that got a 13-year-old girl pregnant. He took off out of state just as fast as he could when he heard she was pregnant. She thought he really loved her. He had told her that he loved her, but didn't want to go to jail and she had promised not to tell. She didn't, but when a 13-year-old girl turns up pregnant at the doctor's office, they are mandated reporters for child abuse and an investigation was initiated. A warrant was put out for him and he was eventually picked up. He claimed, "It wasn't rape". I advised him that it didn't matter if she shook her head yes, because she wasn't old enough to legally consent. In another case we had a girl that I believe was 14-years-old. Her cousin was 19 or 20-years-old. He was really big into one of those fantasy role playing games. Anyway, his cousin liked him and they played this game together, but one day she admitted to a friend that he raped her. The friend told her mother who made a call to the child abuse hotline. When questioned, the girl told how he had hurt her raping her and gave a credible statement which was corroborated by the fact that she had a history of playing this game with her cousin, but one day suddenly stopped and wouldn't have anything to do with him. She was upset at what happened, but still cared enough for him that she didn't want him to go to prison. There hadn't been any witnesses and she had waited too long for there to be any DNA evidence that we could use. He reported being very fond of her, verified that they had played this game quite often, but also very credibly and adamantly denied raping her, but he wasn't able to explain why she suddenly stopped playing the game and didn't want to have anything to do with him. I remember telling him that I wanted to believe him, but I just couldn't get past her suddenly stopping playing the game with him and suddenly not wanting to have anything to do with him without an explanation. I told him that if he could pass a polygraph that would do it to which he agreed. Just then our polygraph examiner was out on medical leave and the nearest examiner was about 3 hours away. Due to a heavy work schedule, they could only do the polygraph if we agreed to transport. I picked the young man up and we started driving. Now imagine a 3 hour drive with someone you believe has forcibly raped his underage teenage cousin… I was sure he had done it, but I also knew it would be impossible to get a conviction based on the evidence we had available. I'd like to take a moment here to strongly encourage anyone that has been assaulted to report it to the police as quickly as possible. I understand it may be difficult, but it is important and may prevent someone else from having to suffer as well. To continue, I said a prayer for God's will on this trip and casually asked more about this game… he spent the next 3 hours very in depth telling me all about this dark elf realm. I realized that he had spent so much time in this game that it had become more real to him than the real world. I also remembered that when I was a Counterintelligence Special Agent there was a very real concern about leaving people under cover for too long as the same thing could happen. The thing that I most remember was him telling me that in this dark elf realm the only law was that you don't get caught and the only punishment for getting caught was death. When we got ready for the polygraph I advised the examiner about the dark elf realm and the only law and the only punishment. When faced with failing the polygraph he broke down and confessed to raping his cousin and was arrested. They put him on suicide watch as he was so into that game there was a real concern he would kill himself; not for the rape, but for getting caught. I love watching God work though… I only learned the key piece of information we needed listening to this young man talk about the dark elf realm for 3 hours. Had our normal examiner not been on medical leave at that exact time we probably wouldn't have gotten enough evidence for him to have been arrested.

ANOTHER CASE INVOLVING ROLE PLAYING GAMES GONE TOO FAR

Thankfully, in this case the mother realized she had a problem and called 911 for help before anything bad happened. She reported hearing voices telling her to harm herself and her children and was admitted for treatment. In this situation the children had been left in the care of their grandparents, but a report was called in for us to assess as the mother was released from in-patient treatment. When I came up to the house I observed boxes of Christian reference books that any minister would have been proud to own stacked in the carport. Inside the home I noted the mother had been playing another of those computer role playing games. Her children told me that she would be playing it all hours of the night. I also noticed that the mother had made a t-shirt of her role playing character that she wore when playing the game. It had occult symbols on it, but she claimed not to know what they were, but just that she had liked them. She was also reading a popular vampire series which was open on the side table next to her chair. You may want to go back and review my chapter on "The Case of The Vampire" for a picture of a real life vampire story.

I asked the mother about the books on the carport and was told that they had belonged to her grandfather who had been a deacon at his church. She said she didn't have room for them in the house. She said she'd thought about getting rid of them, but stacked them on the carport instead. I advised her about the occult symbols on her shirt and recommended that she take it, the computer game and vampire books out and burn them and bring the Christian reference books in the home and read those instead.

In another situation, I received a call from a young woman who had been playing with a Ouija board, but it began to frighten her. I was able to pray with her over the phone and had her take it out and burn it. Ouija boards are sadly sold as toys, but they are actual occult instruments and I'd highly recommend anyone that has one take it out and burn it. As a young Christian I was very fortunate to have attended a serious Bible study involving the occult. I didn't know at the time (but God did) that years later the information I learned in that Bible study I'd be using during child abuse investigations. Today, many teenage girls have been drawn into the occult. They see their own homes and families broken and dysfunctional and are drawn to the occult when they see shows with attractive, strong, successful women who are witches. It is my prayer to see God's Church reaching out to these young ladies in God's love letting them see the real power in Christ Jesus. Sadly, I have had too many (and one would have been too many) young ladies tell me they attended church growing up, but got pregnant as a young teen and were no longer welcome at their church. When they needed the love and support of the church the most, they were instead rejected. I'm not saying that we condone sin, but I am saying that we love the person, and provide an atmosphere where God can heal and restore. Sadly, I've seen churches that want God to clean people before they catch them, but that isn't how it works. We're supposed to reach out and catch them with our love, and then let God clean them in His timing and in His way. Sadly, I also see Christians who think it is up to them to do the cleaning, but do more damage than good, because they didn't allow God to do it in His way and His time. I believe it was Joyce Meyer I heard tell a story of when she was a young Christian that God had called to ministry, but at that time she was wearing short shorts and had a cigarette in one hand and her Bible in the other. If some Christian had not allowed God to develop her in His way and His time, and instead crushed her spirit, she might not have the ministry she does today. I remember a choir teacher when I was still in grade school that laughed and made a comment about my voice breaking at the time. I know she didn't mean it and would be upset if she knew how it affected me, but for years after I wouldn't sing aloud in public. Later, I took a choir class in high school just because I didn't like having fear in my life. We have to be careful of what and how we say things to people. We have to provide an atmosphere of love, acceptance (not of the behavior, but of the person), and forgiveness, and then let God heal and restore people in His time. He is the only one that truly knows a person's whole situation and the best way and timing to heal and restore them.

THE CASE OF THE CONDOM ON
THE SIDE OF THE ROAD

(A former high school big shot gets caught)

In another case, we had a former big shot from high school that graduated, but all of a sudden wasn't such a big deal anymore. I believe he was around 22-years-old when we got involved. He had developed a habit of hanging out at his old high school haunts flirting with underage girls that still looked up to him as a big deal. He would apparently scope out and target a girl, wait till he caught her alone, and then ask her if she'd like to go for a drive. He'd offer her some beer while they were driving. I can hardly tell you how many teenage girls I've had to interview that thought they could take care of themselves, but made a bad decision and as a result ended up over their heads in trouble. Most teenage girls wanting to think they are all grown up are flattered by attention from an "adult man" and are excited to go for a drive alone and to be offered beer; however, this guy would take them out for a drive to a remote area with the only intention of having sex with them. During the investigation I found one other girl that admitted he took her out like that and raped her, but she refused to testify. I'm sure there were others that although underage, were willing and never reported it. In this particular case though, he took out a 14-year-old virgin. She didn't have a father at home, was a loner, and was flattered at his attention. She didn't really want the beer and told me how she didn't like the taste, but took some sips to look grown up. Although she started getting nervous and asked where he was going, she was flattered when he parked and kissed her, but she became fearful and wanted to stop when he started taking off her clothes. It was dark, they were out in the middle of nowhere, and he had enough beers that he wasn't going to stop… he raped her. He tore her up and she was traumatized, but apparently in his mind thinking he had "seduced" this girl… he told her, "It was nice" when he dropped her off (a safe enough distance from her home that he wouldn't be spotted) and asked her how she liked it. I'll never forget her telling me how she just wanted to go home and take as long and as hot a shower as she could. Her mother had been at work and her daughter was supposed to have been home, but her mother could tell something was wrong when she got home and her daughter finally told her what happened. The mother called the police. The medical examiner that conducted the sexual abuse exam was visibly upset at how torn up the girl was. She made the comment, "the tears were bad enough that they still hadn't stopped bleeding". The girl gave a detailed and credible statement, but unfortunately for an arrest, no one saw her picked up or dropped off, and he had taken the time to use a condom. During the interview she mentioned that he threw the condom out the window of the car. She didn't know where they were though when he did it. I got the girl's mother to sit in the back of the car and I used an interview technique I'd learned as a Counterintelligence Special Agent. I had the daughter sit in the front seat of the car and told her that I didn't want her to re-live what happened, but wanted her to imagine that she was watching what happened in a movie. It wasn't happening to her, but she was just watching a movie. I started where she reported being picked up and had her take me turn for turn till all of a sudden out in the middle of nowhere she tensed up and froze. I knew I was where the rape had happened. I pulled off the side of the road, put on the emergency blinkers, and started walking down the road. It wasn't very long before I found the condom. The young man was arrested and initially denied even being with her, but when we showed him the condom in an evidence bag, he admitted that they had sex, but then tried to claim it had been consensual. Because of her age it didn't matter as she was too young, but he had also already been caught lying. We also had the tearing evidence from the prompt sexual abuse exam, but without the condom we probably wouldn't have had enough evidence for a conviction. The "technique" I used to locate the condom was a good technique, but I don't believe it would have been good enough without some leading by The Holy Spirit.

THE YOUNG MAN AT JUVENILIE COURT

(The results of young people being "uninvited" from church)

    This isn't an actual case that I worked, but rather a situation that I came across as a result of my work. I was at court on another case when I recognized a young man from my son's school in juvenile court. I didn't actually recognize him from the school, but because he had attended a youth program that my son had also been in. I knew that this young man's mother and father were divorced and his father didn't have much to do with him even though they didn't live very far apart from each other. I was also aware that even though they were divorced there was still quite a bit of conflict between the mother and father. He, like my son, had been attending a youth program where The Holy Spirit was present and it had been a fast growing youth group… 30 – 50 young people were coming on Wednesdays and Sundays and many young people were being baptized. That was quite a large number of young people for a small community and it was still growing quickly. One of the things that I'll never forget was that the youth of their own accord started doing "the wave" (like at a big sporting event) whenever another youth was baptized. I thought it was great, but then "it" happened… there were people in the church that "didn't think it was very holy that the youth were doing the wave in church", there was also concern over the kind of young people that were starting to come, and when some money turned up missing it was immediately blamed on them. People started criticizing the youth minister and questioning why he was baptizing kids when he hadn't even been to Bible College. When he refused to "un-invite" any of these young people he was asked to step down. Sadly, The Holy Spirit was grieved, and the program fell apart.

The young man in juvenile court had been running with other youth that got in trouble with the law and he ended up in juvenile court about to be sent to juvenile detention. Because of my job, I was allowed to speak with him for a little bit before he was transported. He was hanging his head as I approached and on the verge of tears. He was in an orange jump suit and wearing handcuffs that also attached to his legs to prevent him from being able to run away. My heart was deeply saddened. I asked him if he knew who I was and he did. I also asked him if he knew my son and he did. I told him that when he was released from juvenile detention that my son would be a good friend to him… that was when it hit me… this situation was the Bible in a nutshell… all of us apart from God are just juveniles in trouble with the law, but our Heavenly Father is saying, "Do you know my Son? He'd be a good friend to you." I was allowed to say a quick prayer over him and give him some Christian tracts that I had on me to take with him as he was taken away.

I asked him if he knew who I was and he did. I also asked him if he knew my son and he did. I told him that when he was released from juvenile detention that my son would be a good friend to him… that was when it hit me… this situation was the Bible in a nutshell… all of us apart from God are just juveniles in trouble with the law, but our Heavenly Father is saying, "Do you know my Son? He'd be a good friend to you."

THE FAMILY IN POVERTY

(An opportunity for God's Church to make a difference)

Sometimes we get involved in cases that aren't actually child abuse, but poverty. There is a difference. However, when we run into cases where children are on the verge of improper care due to poverty we assess the situation and attempt to direct the family to resources which can help get them on track. I remember a particular case where the parents had been working, both in very low income jobs, but had been managing to barely hold it together. They had a large number of children from previous marriages (his, hers, ours). I'm not going to mention the exact number to help not identify the family. Anyway, the father lost his job due to a decline in the economy and wasn't able to find another that he was capable of doing in a rural area. Things that were already just barely hanging on began to spiral downward quickly. They couldn't afford their car insurance, couldn't renew their vehicle registration without insurance, and got a ticket for driving an improperly registered vehicle. They couldn't afford the ticket and got in trouble for unpaid fines. They didn't have any family they could turn to and weren't members of a church that could have helped. The city code enforcement officer told me he really should have condemned their house, but knew they were in poverty and knew if he did they wouldn't have anyplace else to live. We opened a case, provided some emergency supplies, and began the slow process of helping get the family back on solid footing, but I remember a thought that I believe was God inspired that crossed my mind while I was helping provide emergency services to help prevent having to take their kids in foster care. I thought wouldn't it be wonderful if I had a list of available area churches that had put together a "Helps Urgent Response Team", (a HURT team) that was prepared not to give money, but to really invest in coming in and loving and help get a family back on track. A group of church members that have committed to being available one Saturday a month to respond when a family in their congregation's area (and not just for members) is in need of help. I know churches get deluged with requests for emergency funds. It is financially and mentally draining for the churches and in my opinion not often a good idea for the family either. Once in awhile someone might just need a little help to cover something they couldn't avoid, but oftentimes what they really need is what we call "intensive family services" to help correct what is causing the problem in the first place. Often these families were never taught by example how to be successful families, but imagine if a "Helps Urgent Response Team" shows up early on a Saturday morning; not in condemnation, but in Christ's love. A Youth Team works with the children while ladies of the church help the mother and the men of the church work with the father. This is real, roll up your sleeves, getting dirty, in the trenches Christian love. No strings attached, but I'd be willing to bet that family would be drawn to that kind of love. I know of a church that started reaching out to kids in foster care. There are 2 families in that church now that were former foster kids. They grew up, got married, have kids themselves, and all of them are baptized, regularly attending members. I understand that the parent of one of those children has started attending also!

THE CASE OF THE TEENAGER WHO "AGED OUT" OF THE SYSTEM

(Another opportunity for God's Church to make a difference)

When a young person turns 18 in the foster care system they aren't just put out on their own. There is a program called the independent living program that helps prepare them to be out on their own. It includes life skills, trades or college training, and follow up assistance by a caseworker; however, once a person turns 18 they can't be forced to stay in the program. I always strongly encourage young people to stay in the program until they are really prepared to be on their own. I've been in court when these young people were in front of the judge requesting their case to be closed and for them to be on their own. I've heard the judge strongly encourage them to stay until they were really ready, but at 18, they can't be forced to stay and many make a very big mistake and get out before they are really ready. I remember a young man just like that. He was a likeable young man and I actually met him after he "aged out" of the foster care system. He had been a witness in another case that I was working. After he turned 18 and had requested out of the system he did okay for awhile, but he didn't have any family or church support. He lost his job, lost his place, and was pretty much staying with whoever would take him in. He liked me and knew I was good for a snack and soda out of the vending machine if he saw my car. I spent numerous hours trying to find a program that was appropriate for him. My supervisor finally did in another state and even made arrangements for him to be taken there. We were surprised when some time later he showed back up in town. He had decided to leave the program and hitched his way back to town. He was an easy target for the wrong kind of people to take advantage of and finally ended up in trouble with the law. He was liked by local law enforcement who really didn't want to have to arrest him, but I remember them telling me, "Chris, at least here he has three square meals a day, a shower, clean clothes, and a safe place to sleep". Actually, he liked the law enforcement officers and really didn't mind being in the County lock up. Unfortunately he got in bigger trouble later on in another county and ended up being sent to prison. I tried calling and finding someway to help, but he'd gotten into enough trouble this time that I couldn't. I have kept him in prayer often though. I remember thinking at the time how much I wished there was some church that could have taken him under their wing. Maybe made a room for him in exchange for helping keep the church clean and had some retired person that might have enjoyed the company and making a difference to have kept an eye on him and kept him out of trouble. I remember another situation where the mother was working and when the father wasn't in jail he was an alcoholic and not much help to the family anyway. The teenage kids were home alone after school and the house had become a thorn in the neighborhood's side. It was where all the juveniles would hand out after school and get in trouble, because there was no adult supervision. When I approached the house I remember looking down the street on the right side and seeing a church. I looked down the street on the left side and saw another church. I remember thinking couldn't one of these churches be open for a few hours everyday after school, so the kids had a place they could go after school to get some cheap cookies and Kool-Aid and do their homework and maybe play some games under the supervision of a caring retired adult. I'm sure there are lonely retired people out there that would love to have a place to go everyday where they were needed and could make a difference. They might worry if they were "qualified" to do that, but the only qualification would be that they care and prayed. When my son Adam was old enough to walk home alone from the school, we were blessed to have a lovely elderly Christian neighbor that watched for him everyday till he got home from the bus. He was old enough, but we still didn't think it was good for him to just be alone till we got home from work. It was a blessing for us, for him, and I also believe for her. For those readers out there who mistakenly think they are "too old" to still make a difference, I'd like to share another story. Many years ago, when my son was still very little, he caught a very bad virus and his temperature shot up frighteningly. I was a night shift supervisor at the time and was sleeping before I had to leave for work when my wife Jackie rushed in saying, "Chris, quick, there is something wrong with the baby!" He had a dangerously high fever and was unresponsive. Jackie and I rushed to get his fever down and race him to the hospital emergency room. In our hurry, we didn't grab any of his stuffed animals. The doctors were quick to get his temperature under control, but he was frightened in the hospital and uncomfortable until a nurse brought over a little stuffed bear for him to hold. The bear was roughly cut from rags and hand sewn. It wasn't much to look at. One side was from an old flannel shirt and the other looked like it came from the lining of an old jacket. The eyes were two other scrap pieces that had been stitched on, but he loved it and quickly fell asleep holding it. I asked the nurse who I should thank for the bear, but she claimed not to know, saying only that an elderly woman had anonymously donated a number of the bears.

Even after Adam was home from the hospital, the bear was his favorite and was seldom far from his reach. Eventually though, the little bear was washed one too many times and fell apart. Adam was older by then and moved on to "big boy" toys, but the little bear had helped him at a very difficult time and I never forgot it. I often think about the woman that lovingly made and donated the bear. I would say a prayer for her and wonder what had led her to make such an anonymous gift. I'll most likely never know her story in this life, but I learned we can all make a difference in someone's life if we look at what we have instead of what we don't. Many may have looked at that elderly woman and mistakenly thought she didn't have anything important left to offer, but how many families have been touched by some old rags that were lovingly sewn together?

THE CASE OF THE "SQUIRTING TURTLE"

(Don't jump to conclusions)

As I mentioned earlier, whenever I went out on a new case I always had two prayers. The first was that I wanted to ensure any kid was safe. The second was that I wanted to ensure that no one was wrongly accused. We had a case where there was a bitter divorce and custody case. When the child, a very little girl, came home from her first visit at daddy's new house, she told mommy about playing with "daddy's squirting turtle in the bathtub". Immediately the mother was in a rage, rallied all her forces, and was at the police station filing a complaint. A good first interview (especially with a young child) is crucial and I was called in to assist. The little girl repeated her story about playing with daddy's squirting turtle in the bathtub. I realized; however, during the initial interview that the little girl hadn't been abused and what she was describing was a tub toy. We went to the father's house and verified it. He had wanted to ensure his little girl had a good first visit and had bought her some toys including a "squirting turtle" tub toy. The allegation was quickly "unsubstantiated". We hadn't disclosed any information and provided notice that the report had been unsubstantiated; however, sadly the damage had been done. I'm sure that all the premature allegations made by the mother and her family and friends wrongly labeled the man. Sadly, there are probably still family and friends that are just sure he really did something wrong.

I shared that as a lead in to this next situation. It is a situation that I prayed especially hard over before sharing due to the extremely disturbing nature. Ultimately though I felt there was an important message that needed to be shared. We had a case involving an infant that had been sexually abused. While the baby's diaper was being changed, a family member observed that "something was wrong" with the baby's vagina. It was actually very clear that the infant had been sexually abused. The young mother's live-in boyfriend was immediately suspected as he was the only male that had access to the baby. Not jumping to conclusions though and working the investigation, we were shocked to discover that it was actually the baby's mother that had "sexually" abused the infant baby. The mother confessed, was arrested, and the baby taken into protective custody. The reason that I ultimately shared this disturbing case was that during the investigation, we discovered that while this young mother was still a child, although a little older than the other girl, she was invited to a birthday party at the girl's house who had been traded for drugs by her stepfather. The stepfather had gotten this girl apart, given her alcohol, and sexually molested her. She never told anyone, but it messed her up. Apparently, she had become so messed up sexually that she was putting a hairbrush handle among other things into her own little baby's vagina. I don't know that we ever found out who the actual biological father of the baby was. It hadn't been the mother's live-in boyfriend. I do know that the little baby was beautiful and adopted by a loving family (thank God). I hope that this young mother is able to find The Lord while she is in prison and find healing for herself also. The reason for sharing this was to show the continuing cycle of abuse that occurs and the absolute need to somehow break that cycle. The only way that I know to break that cycle is for the church to rise up, reach out in love (and that is hard core Christianity in action in a case like this), and provide the environment necessary for God to heal these families.

THE ABSCONDED SEX OFFENDER

(A worse place than prison)

In this case there were two little girls with developmental delays that began acting out sexually in their special education class. I was called in to interview the girls. The youngest girl was very young and too developmentally delayed to have much of an interview. The elder sister was still pretty young as well and also developmentally delayed, but I was able to get enough during the interview that I was confident her stepfather was most probably molesting her and arranged for an immediate sexual abuse exam. We were very blessed to have the sexual abuse examiner that we did. She was very committed to the children, was a great witness in court, and had actually written the chapter in the medical book on juvenile sexual abuse exams. The prosecuting attorneys and juries loved that in court and the defense attorneys didn't! I've previously expressed my appreciation for the medical personnel involved in these cases, but I'd like to go a little further here. It is extremely difficult on the medical examiners in these cases. First, they are constantly dealing with children that have been sexually abused. Second, they themselves get abused in court. The first trick in a defense attorney's tool bag is to harass the medical examiner. They do this by coming in the day the prosecutor is prepared for trial and has the medical examiner present to testify and request a continuance. This is difficult for everyone involved including the victim and their family, but most especially for the medical examiner. It would be great if states could afford full time medical examiners on state payroll that just do these exams and testify in court, but that would be a big expense to taxpayers; so typically, the medical examiner is a doctor or nurse practitioner with their own practices that have taken it upon themselves to pursue special training and certification to conduct sexual abuse exams. When they are subpoenaed to appear in court and testify at the trial they are not at their practice earning a living and are inconveniencing their other patients. It is very difficult and costly for them to take a day out of their medical practices (for only a token witness fee) and then have to come back again. I've never been aware of a case where the defense wasn't allowed at least one continuance. I understand it is because they would use that as grounds for an appeal. They'll sometimes even get a second continuance. If at any of these court dates; however, the defense attorney doesn't see the key prosecution witnesses (especially a medical examiner), they will want to go for the trial then and try to get that evidence thrown out, because they can't challenge them in court. I remember a particular case just like that... at the second trial attempt we hadn't been able to locate the examiner for the trial. The defense attorney wanted to proceed and try to get the medical evidence thrown out which would have drastically injured the case. We were doing everything to track down the examiner. Thank God we were able to at the last minute and won the case. The examiner had been recovering from surgery themselves at a family member's home, but came in to testify anyway (a true hero to children)! I'm going to add here that I know a really good defense attorney that came to me and said he wasn't going to be able to defend these cases anymore. He had just became a new father and said he made his decision the first time he held his new baby girl in his arms. He took a substantial earnings cut to be a prosecuting attorney for the state (another hero to children)! I'm going to take another moment here to go out on a limb and say why I don't like the show "CSI"... don't get me wrong; it is a very well done and entertaining show. My wife loves it. I'm also sure that all the equipment they show is available somewhere; however, in the normal real world, no local law enforcement agency has that kind of money, equipment, and personnel. If anyone that ever reads this book is ever on a jury please forget everything you ever saw on "CSI" and realize that almost no local law enforcement agency has that kind of money, equipment, and personnel. I pray that one day they all do, but in the normal world, crime labs are so overworked we have to wait months for results (not 45 minutes to finish the show on time). Also, investigators typically have very heavy caseloads (another reason everyone that does this work protecting kids is a hero in my book) and can't afford 4 people working on just one case! Anyway, getting back to this case... the examiner in this case was visibly shocked and physically upset when she began the exam. Normally, a sexual abuse exam is a very intrusive exam that is difficult for a grown woman not to mention children, but in this case, the second the little girl was placed on the exam table she immediately spread her legs and everything opened up wide. Her little body had been so sexually abused, that for protection it had trained itself to be quickly prepared for sexual activity even though her body had not yet been through puberty and estrogenized. Prior to puberty and a girl's body becoming estrogenized, sexual penetration would be painful. This is why in many of these type cases there won't be actual evidence of penetration, but only irritation on the outside if caught quickly enough. Defense attorneys often try to claim in the defense that there wasn't any evidence of penetration and that is why. In this case the girl also made a corroborating statement to the examiner and deputies went out to pick up the stepfather. When they arrived they found the man dead in his truck. He had duct taped a dryer hose to his truck's tailpipe and into his window. He sealed the gap in the window with duct tape, started the truck, and asphyxiated himself. During the investigation it was determined that he was an absconded sex offender from another state. Instead of registering in his state as a sex offender and complying with his parole, he met the mother of these children on the internet and quickly maneuvered his way into marrying her and moving in with her (and the little girls) out-of-state. When we called the other state to let them know that we found one of their absconded sex offenders and they had committed suicide; I remember them saying, "Good work, he saved everyone a trial... guess he didn't want to go back to prison"... I remember thinking just then that after getting a look at hell; he was probably wishing he could just go back to prison. This man needed to go back to prison, but I hate for anyone to go to hell.

I wanted to use this opportunity to caution people about the internet. I've been involved in a number of cases where the mother met the offender over the internet. Also, I don't know of any of these offenders that didn't have a major internet porn addiction. Sadly, too many of our teenage girls today are playing dangerous games on the internet. I remember a particular case where a teenage girl had developed a relationship with a man over the internet. She had uploaded pictures of herself in just her panties in her bedroom in risqué poses. I believe we had been notified of the situation by a friend who was worried for her friend's safety (she was a good friend). The parents initially refused to even acknowledge that it was possible that their little girl had done this, but agreed for us to take a quick look at her computer in her bedroom. Just a cursory check quickly found where she had been playing a very dangerous game flirting with a man on-line. Her parents had to admit that their little girl hadn't been as innocent on the computer as they had believed. This book isn't about internet security (that is another whole book), but I would like to stress to parents not to be naïve about the dangers of the internet and to ensure they take appropriate protective measures such as porn blocking programs and keeping the computer in an area where someone won't be tempted to do things they shouldn't. For the students who think they are being smart and not giving enough information that someone could track them down (that is what the girl above thought), we were quickly able to show her how easy it was to identify her location based on innocent enough information she had provided such as the name of their high school team, colors, and mascot among others. I mentioned earlier that I had been a counterintelligence special agent. There are people that put together all kinds of intelligence information based on accumulating enough "innocent" information over time.

EPILOGUE

I wanted to end this book with a couple of happy endings and a word about our ministry, "Reach Out Christ's Kingdom" (R.O.C.K.) Ministries, but there are just a few more cases I didn't want to make whole separate chapters, but did want to touch on as they are things I've seen while out working cases that warrant sharing.

In one situation, I was following up on a mother who married a registered sex offender. Child Protective Services stepped in when notified by his parole officer to ensure the safety of an adolescent daughter she had. She had signed over guardianship of her daughter to a grandmother in order to marry a registered sex offender. She could visit her daughter, but her daughter was not to be in the home. I was sent to ensure the mother was complying. She was cooperative and walked me through her house, but I felt led to actually check the closets as well. Sure enough, I found the mother had the daughter in the home and hid her in the back of one of the closets, so she wouldn't be caught violating the safety plan. A protective hold was placed on the daughter. The mother was charged with child endangerment and her husband was reported to his parole officer. She later testified that her husband (registered sex offender) left her as soon as the daughter was taken into protective custody. I see so many women that meet registered sex offenders (very often over the internet) and don't believe he did it, or that he would do it with her child. I tell them I hope he didn't do it, but he has to deal with the fact that he IS registered, and he knows what his restrictions are and that he is putting her custody in jeopardy and risking going back to jail himself being around her child. No woman should marry a man that is willing to do that whether he did it or not. I'm going to add though that while no mother should chose anyone over her children, that they would still be welcome at our ministry. I know of churches that have asked registered sex offenders to not come there, but how are we ever going to heal people and break cycles if they can't attend a church. Now, I'm not going to have them unsupervised or behaving improperly, but I wouldn't leave an alcoholic alone with a bottle of alcohol either. I've always considered that a church should be a spiritual hospital and people can't be helped if they're not allowed in the doors.

While talking about doing a thorough walkthrough of homes, I was responding to another child abuse Hotline report and really wasn't seeing where the children were being abused or neglected, but it was also clear there was something the family didn't want me to see. It isn't uncommon for child abuse investigators to walk in on other illegal activity. The number one reason we get involved is usually over drugs. They reluctantly took me through the house where in a back bedroom I found grandma tied in her wheelchair with her urine bag overflowing. She wasn't tied in as a prisoner, but to keep her from falling out of her chair. I called for assistance and uniformed officers arrived with an ambulance and adult protective services. The parents had been keeping grandma at home to continue to cash her social security checks. I took a protective hold on the children and adult protective services placed a protective hold on the grandmother who was taken to the hospital. The parents were arrested.

I just mentioned that drugs are often the leading cause for child protective services to be called. In another case along those lines, the neighbors hadn't seen the mother or her child for a couple of days and there was a terrible odor around the door of the house. I responded to a report called in to the hotline and contacted local police who got authorization to force the door based on the situation. When the door opened, we were hit in the face with what smelled like a dead body. Mom was passed out on the couch on drugs, in her own excrement. We couldn't wake her and an ambulance was called. Her two-year-old was running around filthy and naked, apparently living off old leftover fast food strewn around the filthy home. A protective hold was taken. This is probably a good place to mention that I always carry an emergency kit in my car that includes a first aid kit, disinfectant wipes, bug spray, dog treats, and some Vicks vapor rub. The Vicks was passed around for under noses while everyone did what they had to do. I was wearing a leather coat and concerned if the smell would come out.

In another case of a filthy home, the mother told me she could live any way that she chose and I didn't have any right to tell her otherwise. I told her I didn't have any say in how SHE lived, but when she brought a child into it, the child's safety WAS my business!

I hate drugs, because of what I've seen it do to families. In another case the mother was arrested for drugs and I was called out over her two daughters. I told the two young teen girls that I was going to be taking them to a foster home for awhile and to gather up a few things. They each grabbed a large trash bag which was all their possessions. What struck me as especially sad (beside all they had was readily in a large trash bag) was how matter of fact they were about it. To them, this was normal.

In another case, I was out checking on children, but was suspicious of outbuildings on the property and uncovered the worst case of animal cruelty in the county. The mother had a puppy mill, but the animals hadn't been fed or watered and had even resorted to eating dogs that had died. A protective hold was placed on the children and the mother was charged with sixty counts of animal cruelty.

Why did I share these last incidents? Because, it shows that child abuse isn't a separate and isolated situation, but often tied with animal and adult abuse and drugs and pornography as well. When going through State training to be an investigator, we are trained to do "holistic" assessments where we look at the whole situation. I believe that the number one cause of all these problems is the breakdown of the family. I also believe that the State can help and treat symptoms, but only God can heal individuals and families. This is the purpose of "Reach Out Christ's Kingdom (R.O.C.K.) Ministries". In Luke 1:17 (KJV), The Bible says, "And he shall go before him in the spirit and power of Elias, to turn the hearts of the fathers to the children, and the disobedient to the wisdom of the just; to make ready a people prepared for the Lord." That verse probably best expresses the mission of ROCK... reaching out, turning the hearts of the fathers to the children...

Okay, I said I was going to end on some happy endings...

In one case, we had a foster child who had extreme anger issues... he had disrupted his current placement by tearing up the fixtures out of a bathroom and was being placed inpatient treatment, but his caseworker was afraid of him and I was asked to transport. I told the young man that we had a long drive, but I had some Christian comics in the back seat if he'd like to read them. He cursed, "I'm not reading any comics, and I'm sure not reading any Christian comics!" I told him it was his choice and started driving. After awhile he became bored and quietly started looking at the Christian comics. Sometime later I got a call from his caseworker stating he asked if I had anymore of those comics which I sent over.

A little while later I got a call from his caseworker stating that he was asking if I had a Bible he could have which I also sent over. About another month later his caseworker called me and said, "Chris, that young man has joined a church and has not only turned his own life around, but has been making a big difference in his own family also!" (Praise God!)

Lastly, one day a professional looking young woman knocked on my office door... she said you don't recognize me, but I was the young lady passed out on the couch (above) on drugs... she said that she had completed rehab, joined a church, and had turned her life around. She said she was getting her child back that day! (Again, praise God!)

In closing, when I was in grade school I volunteered as a school safety ensuring the younger children made it to school safely. In high school I was a lifeguard and volunteered teaching swimming to physically challenged children. In the Army I was an Infantry Squad Leader and then Counterintelligence Special Agent. As a young Christian I wondered what God was preparing me for. Little did I know I would one day be a Child Abuse Investigator and Minister. As a Child Abuse Investigator I can help one person/family at a time which is a good thing, but as a minister I have the opportunity to inspire a congregation of people at a time to help. With this book I can try to inspire many churches to help lots of people at a time. My intent with this book was not to just write about a bunch of bad situations, but to inspire you to make a difference where you are. So many times people think they can't make a difference, but Jesus said in John 14:12 (KJV), "Verily, verily, I say unto you, He that believeth on me, the works that I do shall he do also; and greater works than these shall he do; because I go unto my Father." It is my prayer that this book has inspired you to reach out in love, acceptance (not of the behavior, but of the person), and forgiveness sharing Jesus to a hurting world. When I was praying in court for the answer, God showed me that we have to share Jesus. He is the answer! Thank you for taking this time with me and God bless!

Pastor Chris Shelton
(If you'd like to learn more about or follow our ministry, you're invited to www.ReachOutChristsKingdom.org)

CONCLUSION

My purpose for sharing these stories with you has been to open the eyes of the Church to situations that are around them everyday to help. The girl that was traded for drugs was attending school everyday in a good community, but no one had a clue of what was actually going on in her life. I'm not claiming that anyone should have known, just that we need to realize that there are people all around us everyday who need us to show them God's love and to be open to The Holy Spirit's leading to do just that. We never know when being obedient to The Holy Spirit's leading when the simplest gesture can change someone's life for eternity. Everyone recognizes the Billy Grahams, but I always think of the faithful Sunday school teacher who leads those people to the Lord. People today are desperate for a real experience with God and not just more religion. Our ministry, "Reach Out Christ's Kingdom" (ROCK) Ministries, is dedicated first to reaching out to those in our own area who have come from difficult backgrounds; not in condemnation or trying to "fix" them, but providing an atmosphere where God can "heal" them. We'll also be concentrating on sharing that mission with others in the Church. I also want to share the idea of each church prayerfully seeking a member in their own congregation to prayerfully support just as they would any foreign missionary that could minister to kids in their area by being a foster parent. There is a desperate need for foster parents and shouldn't the church be the first to respond to this opportunity to truly share God's love? I have a vision for our own area that we'll have more Christian foster homes than we can fill (thank God) and other counties will be coming in and using them; that the church will be so active reaching out and healing families with "Helps Urgent Response Teams" that child abuse reports will become few and far between, and that the Governor of our State will have to take notice of what is making the difference and that it will spread across the State and then our Country and World. In Jesus name... amen.

P.S. When writing this book I guess I first imagined that the majority of readers would be Christians already, but as I close this book out it dawns on me that perhaps some people will be drawn to it that haven't already had a personal experience with Jesus Christ. Perhaps, some people will be reading it that aren't already Christians, but were drawn to the book because they were either in a field that is involved in child protective services, had been abused, or were abusers themselves (or both). I've served in the Army, been a Counterintelligence Special Agent, and spent over 8 years in child protective services, but I've never done anything more important than sharing Jesus Christ with someone. I hope this book has shared Jesus' love throughout, and if you weren't already a Christian hopefully you are ready now to accept Jesus Christ as your personal savior and Lord. The Bible says that <u>we have all sinned and come short of the Glory of God</u> (Rom. 3:23). It also says that <u>the penalty for that sin is death and separation from God</u> (Rom. 6:23), **but God loved us so much** that he became a man, lived a perfect life, and then allowed himself to pay the penalty for our sins (crucified on a cross), so that we could be together with him forever (John 3:16). Now that's love! The Bible says that if you want to accept that love and forgiveness all you have to do is:

1. Believe in your heart that Jesus was the son of God, that he loved you enough to die in your place, and that God raised him from the dead showing his power over death, and then:

2. Confess that belief with you mouth (Rom. 10: 9 & 10). Say out loud right now, "Jesus. I believe that you are the son of God. I believe that you loved me enough to become a man, live a perfect life, and then suffer a terrible death in my place, so that I can be forgiven and live with you forever. Jesus, I'm sorry for my sin, I make you Lord of my life now and ask you to come into my life, fill me with your Holy Spirit and help me become the person that you want me to be. Thank you.

If you've just done that then you have a new life in Jesus and the angels in heaven are rejoicing (It says so in Luke 15:10). Take time to talk with God each day in prayer (it doesn't have to and shouldn't be fancy "religious" talk. He has called you His friend now, so speak with him like the most loving, worthy friend you could ever have), get and read your Bible each day to learn more about God (He will speak to you through His Word), your new life (and the benefits that come with it), and find a good Bible believing church to attend (you'll gain strength through having friendships with fellow Christians). God bless you as you share the good news of Jesus Christ and His love.

RECOMMENDED READING

(Some other books that Chris recommends)

"Love, Acceptance, & Forgiveness" (Equipping the Church to be Truly Christian in a Non-Christian World), by Jerry Cook with Stanley Baldwin – This book is used as a textbook at the ministry school I attended and confirmed what I had been feeling in the Spirit. Our ministry, "Reach Out Christ's Kingdom" (ROCK) Ministries, will always strive to be, "An Oasis of Love, Acceptance, & Forgiveness" as described in this book.

"In His Steps", by Charles Sheldon – Written in 1896, this is a life changing book, and where the saying "What Would Jesus Do" came from. When I finally found this book I was upset that no Christian had ever shown it to me before.

"The Autobiography of George Mueller" - (27 September 1805 – 10 March 1898), A Christian evangelist depending solely on God in prayer that cared for and provided educations to over 10,000 orphans in his lifetime; another life changing book and testament to the power of prayer.

"Life, In Spite of Me", by Kristen Jane Anderson with Tricia Goyer – After losing several friends and her grandmother within two years, and being raped by a friend she thought she could trust, Kristen slipped into depression and attempted suicide on a set of railroad tracks. Although losing her legs, she miraculously survived to learn of a God who loved her and had a good plan for her life. She completed Bible college and founded a ministry reaching out to others battling depression (www.ReachingYou.org). I've referred this book to many facing depression following abuse.

WHAT TO DO IF YOU'VE BEEN ABUSED

1. Report it as quickly as possible… I understand and appreciate this is a difficult thing to do. The one young lady I spoke about earlier said that all she wanted to do was go home and take as long and hot a shower as she could, but fortunately for her she had a mother who was concerned and encouraged her. The early interview and sexual abuse exam allowed us to obtain the evidence needed for a prosecution. Sadly, the investigation revealed another girl that the same thing had happened to, but she refused to report it. If she had, possibly the second rape may have been avoided. Additionally, prompt medical attention may help prevent a disease and can help provide other services such as counseling. If you aren't fortunate enough to have a trusted family member you can confide in, tell someone else who can help such as a teacher, police officer, nurse, or coach. All of these are "mandated reporters" who will notify a child abuse hotline. Unfortunately, I remember a case where a grandmother who had custody told her granddaughter, "What happens in the family stays in the family". The granddaughter was taken into foster care and the grandparents arrested, because the girl told a teacher who notified the child abuse hotline.

2. Get good counseling… I tell everyone that has been offended on (I don't personally like the connotation of the word victim) that what happened to them was NOT their fault (it was the fault of the

offender) and although they can't change what happened in the past, they have a choice as to what happens now and the future. They can either allow what happened to continue to control them which just continues the abuse (or worse, the cycle of abuse), or they can choose to overcome what happened and even use that to help others as well. You are NOT *"what"* has happened to you. You ARE what you choose to be. In Judges 6:12, God calls Gideon a mighty man of valor although at that point Gideon calls himself poor and the least in his father's house, but God says, Surely I will be with thee and Gideon goes on to be one of the heroes of the Bible. It IS important what you say about yourself. You are NOT a victim! You ARE an overcomer! A good counselor can help. I personally recommend finding a good Christian counselor. I was very blessed when a young woman came up to me at a training seminar and said I didn't remember her, but I had responded to her home years before and while there had given her a Bible and encouraged her. She said she was excited to learn that I was attending the training, because she wanted to let me know that she had went to college and was now a social worker. I really appreciated that, or when I get a phone call from the jail from someone who accepted the Lord because of Christian comics and Bibles our ministry has given out at the jail.

3. Forgive. Not because they deserve it, but because you do. Don't get me wrong... I'm not saying what they did should be excused or that they shouldn't have to account to the law for their crime. You'll remember earlier when I told the man that had molested his daughter that what he did was wrong and he needed to go to jail... What I am saying is that you don't want to imprison yourself as well, but in hate. Hate is like a cancer. Don't allow what happened in the past to destroy your future as well, and don't let hate do it either. You may ask why a loving God allows bad things to happen. Well, that is another book, but let me say here that if something isn't good, it isn't of God, but if we turn to and trust God, He will take something that

was meant to harm us and make something good come out of it. On our ministry website, www.ReachOutChristsKingdom.org I have posted an article I wrote titled, "Why I Believe". It is free and helps explain why bad things happen to good people. I hope you'll check it out and drop me a line if anything I've shared helped. God bless you! If anyone is reading this who has offended on someone and is currently in jail, just like I told the man above, you can be freer in jail with Jesus than out of jail without Him, and if you repent and turn your life over to Jesus, He can use you also and still make something good come out of your life as well! Cheryl Lynn has written another small book with a big message titled, "Ministering Victory Over Abuse". My book, "It's Okay, You're With My Father" is written from the perspective of a Christian child abuse investigator. Cheryl's book is written from the perspective of an overcomer of abuse. I personally think her book should be mandatory reading for all child protective workers. She talks more about emotional healing and I'd highly recommend getting a copy!

APPENDIX

(Recognizing Child Abuse and Neglect: Signs and Symptoms –
*excerpted from U.S. Department of Health & Human Services
Administration for Children & Families website www.childwelfare.gov)*

The first step in helping abused or neglected children is learning to recognize the signs of child abuse and neglect. The presence of a single sign does not prove child abuse is occurring in a family, but a closer look at the situation may be warranted when these signs appear repeatedly or in combination.

If you do suspect a child is being harmed, reporting your suspicions may protect the child and get help for the family. Any concerned person can report suspicions of child abuse and neglect. Some people (typically certain types of professionals) are required by law to make a report of child maltreatment under specific circumstances—these are called mandatory reporters. For more information, see the Child Welfare Information Gateway publication, _Mandatory Reporters of Child Abuse and Neglect_.

For more information about where and how to file a report, contact your local child protective services agency or police department. An additional resource for information and referral is the Childhelp® National Child Abuse Hotline (800.4.A.CHILD).

Recognizing Child Abuse

The following signs may signal the presence of child abuse or neglect.

The Child:

Shows sudden changes in behavior or school performance

Has not received help for physical or medical problems brought to the parents' attention

Has learning problems (or difficulty concentrating) that cannot be attributed to specific physical or psychological causes

Is always watchful, as though preparing for something bad to happen

Lacks adult supervision

Is overly compliant, passive, or withdrawn

Comes to school or other activities early, stays late, and does not want to go home

The Parent:

Shows little concern for the child

Denies the existence of—or blames the child for—the child's problems in school or at home

Asks teachers or other caregivers to use harsh physical discipline if the child misbehaves

Sees the child as entirely bad, worthless, or burdensome

Demands a level of physical or academic performance the child cannot achieve

Looks primarily to the child for care, attention, and satisfaction of emotional needs

The Parent and Child:

Rarely touch or look at each other

Consider their relationship entirely negative

State that they do not like each other

Types of Abuse

The following are some signs often associated with particular types of child abuse and neglect: physical abuse, neglect, sexual abuse, and emotional abuse. It is important to note, however, that these types of abuse are more typically found in combination than alone. A physically abused child, for example, is often emotionally abused as well, and a sexually abused child also may be neglected.

Signs of Physical Abuse
Consider the possibility of physical abuse when the **child**:
Has unexplained burns, bites, bruises, broken bones, or black eyes
Has fading bruises or other marks noticeable after an absence from school
Seems frightened of the parents and protests or cries when it is time to go home
Shrinks at the approach of adults
Reports injury by a parent or another adult caregiver
Consider the possibility of physical abuse when the **parent or other adult caregiver**:
Offers conflicting, unconvincing, or no explanation for the child's injury
Describes the child as "evil," or in some other very negative way
Uses harsh physical discipline with the child
Has a history of abuse as a child

Signs of Neglect
Consider the possibility of neglect when the **child**:
Is frequently absent from school
Begs or steals food or money
Lacks needed medical or dental care, immunizations, or glasses
Is consistently dirty and has severe body odor
Lacks sufficient clothing for the weather

Abuses alcohol or other drugs

States that there is no one at home to provide care

Consider the possibility of neglect when the **parent or other adult caregiver**:

Appears to be indifferent to the child

Seems apathetic or depressed

Behaves irrationally or in a bizarre manner

Is abusing alcohol or other drugs

Signs of Sexual Abuse

Consider the possibility of sexual abuse when the **child**:

Has difficulty walking or sitting

Suddenly refuses to change for gym or to participate in physical activities

Reports nightmares or bedwetting

Experiences a sudden change in appetite

Demonstrates bizarre, sophisticated, or unusual sexual knowledge or behavior

Becomes pregnant or contracts a venereal disease, particularly if under age 14

Runs away

Reports sexual abuse by a parent or another adult caregiver

Consider the possibility of sexual abuse when the **parent or other adult caregiver**:

Is unduly protective of the child or severely limits the child's contact with other children, especially of the opposite sex

Is secretive and isolated

Is jealous or controlling with family members

Signs of Emotional Maltreatment

Consider the possibility of emotional maltreatment when the **child**:

Shows extremes in behavior, such as overly compliant or demanding behavior, extreme passivity, or aggression

Is either inappropriately adult (parenting other children, for example) or inappropriately infantile (frequently rocking or head-banging, for example)

Is delayed in physical or emotional development

Has attempted suicide

Reports a lack of attachment to the parent

Consider the possibility of emotional maltreatment when the **parent or other adult caregiver**:

Constantly blames, belittles, or berates the child

Is unconcerned about the child and refuses to consider offers of help for the child's problems

Overtly rejects the child

Resources on the Child Welfare Information Gateway Website

Child Abuse and Neglect

www.childwelfare.gov/can/

Defining Child Abuse and Neglect

www.childwelfare.gov/can/defining/

Preventing Child Abuse and Neglect

www.childwelfare.gov/preventing/

Reporting Child Abuse and Neglect

www.childwelfare.gov/responding/reporting.cfm

THE REACH OUT CHRIST'S KINGDOM (R.O.C.K.) MINISTRIES' STORY

I previously shared the story above about the man walking along the river continually pulling drowning people out till he was exhausted himself and couldn't keep going, but another person was running upstream to stop the person who was throwing them in. The story is a little humorous, but also very true. As a child abuse investigator handling over one hundred cases a year for over 9 years, I felt like the man that kept going in the water to pull people out one at a time, but was exhausted myself. Pulling people out is important, but wouldn't it be better to stop the people from being thrown into the water in the first place (break the cycles).

I had prayerfully considered this and had almost talked myself into going for my Master's degree and becoming a professional counselor. I knew I would be good at that as well and could still help people and that was the best choice from a financial earnings aspect, but I also knew in my heart that God was calling me to ministry school. I discussed it with my wife who was supportive of me doing what God called me to do and I enrolled in ministry school. While in ministry school I was still working full time and also taking the maximum five classes a semester. Looking back, I'm not really sure how I did it other than to say it was a God thing. The instructors told me they didn't know why I was pushing myself so hard, because

I was completing a three year program in a little over two years. The only answer I could give was that I felt "a sense of urgency".

Near completion of ministry school, my wife and I were in the church we attended during morning worship when the "Reach Out Christ's Kingdom (R.O.C.K.) message suddenly became crystal clear in my mind. I sat down and started writing the whole message out on the back of a church pamphlet. When my pastor came out he had a large rolled banner and was using it to announce that year's conference theme. When they rolled out the banner, I handed the pamphlet I'd written on to my wife to see. The banner they rolled out said, "Revival of Christ's Kingdom" (ROCK). I didn't know they were going to roll out the theme or what it was. We took it as a confirmation. When I shared the pamphlet to my pastor he agreed and donated the banner to us which is now proudly displayed at our ministry. If anyone would like to see the banner they can go to our website, www.ReachOutChristsKingdom.org and click on the facebook link. The photo is posted at our facebook page.

To make sure I was staying in God's plan, I typed out everything that would be needed for the ministry and started checking off the items as God provided. I never went out asking for anything, but kept it in prayer. I told God that I believed He was calling me to ministry and I trusted Him to supply as long as He wanted me to continue. It wasn't long before everything on the list was checked off except for a building. I'd been putting in a lot of hours and had been missing my regular barber and was in desperate need of a haircut when my wife told me to go to where she got her hair cut. I never made it to that haircut. On the front of the building was a memorial plaque dedicating it to the service of the Lord. The building had originally been a mission outreach in the sixties, later becoming its own church. The church outgrew the building and eventually sold it. The sanctuary had been converted to a woman's fitness center. I had no reason to believe the owner would be interested, but felt

The Holy Spirit telling me to go talk to the owner. The owner told me that I didn't have to introduce myself, that she knew who I was and what I was doing and her only question was where was I two years ago when she was praying for a minister to utilize the space. I strongly suspect her prayer was when I started ministry school and the reason I felt the urgency to complete ministry school as quickly as I did.

We made arrangements for me to take over the space for our first service in March, 2010, but on November 11, 2009 my son was coming home late from college. He had worked late keeping score for some games and swerved to avoid a deer. He wasn't speeding, had his seat belt on, and was fine till he tried coming back onto the road and his left rear tire was caught between the gravel and blacktop. It flipped his Blazer upside down, sliding him into a ditch where he rolled back upright. His phone was thrown in the accident and there wasn't anyone around to help. When the Blazer rolled upside down the weight of the vehicle crushed the glass which was imbedded in his arm and tore up his scalp. His ear had also been amputated. Thank God he had the presence of mind to not panic and tie a shirt from his gym bag around his head to stop the bleeding. The nearest light was a pretty good walk, but he said a prayer and started walking.

The home where he went called 911 and me. That is a phone call you never want to get in the middle of the night. The accident happened at the state line and he had walked back into Missouri for help, so there was some confusion dispatching an ambulance and police. My wife and I made it to where he was before either the ambulance or police. Fortunately, my training was such that I made sure my son was stable. My wife worked for a local hospital and had the emergency room on the phone. When the ambulance arrived I went to look for his ear while they properly bandaged him up. The trooper that arrived on the scene was a close friend that

I had worked child abuse cases with. I believe God sent him to strengthen me.

At the hospital, we were blessed by their top E.R. surgeons... after some time removing broken glass, the doctor got my wife and said there had been a lot of scalp damage and he wasn't sure our son's hair would grow back... God bless my wife, before I could say a word she jumped in with, "NO, In the Name of Jesus my son's hair is growing back"! You can see pictures of my son at our website and facebook page. Before removing the broken glass they ran him through a CAT Scan, but there was a problem... the technician stated that they never had a problem with that machine, but it just suddenly wasn't running properly. I asked if they had another and he said it was at another hospital, but the bigger problem was they had already injected my son and he couldn't be re-injected for so many hours. I said, "So what you're really telling me is that we need THIS machine, right NOW"... he said that was correct. Now I don't recommend doing what I next did lightly, but I felt The Holy Spirit strongly leading me and I laid hands on the machine and prayed, "Father, You know we need THIS machine, right NOW... thank You Lord in Jesus' Name. Amen." I asked the technician to try it again and the machine worked perfectly. He kept saying that he'd never seen anything like that before. As I sat in the chairs outside the CAT Scan room I could feel the strongest presence of angels in the room. In fact, (and I don't say this lightly), I felt The Lord Himself right there.

After the E.R. surgeons had done all they could, they said he really needed an ear specialist, but there was a long wait. Thank God again that they were Christians and had gone to medical school with a top ear specialist who had a practice just 100 miles away. They had his personal number and called him and he made arrangements for us to bring Adam right there. Now it was kind of strange, but he said he normally didn't allow family present, but if we'd be okay, he'd let us stay in the room while he worked, but warned us he'd be cutting to clean up the torn cartilage and lay the foundation for any restoration work. We said we'd be in chairs at the end of the room praying. Adam was medicated pretty heavily, but wasn't put totally out for the procedure. After, he said he heard an angel standing next to him saying into his ear that everything was going to be okay and that this would be a testimony. He said he opened his eyes and saw his mom and me sitting and praying and said he could tell an angel was standing there with a hand on each of us. We were again blessed to be referred to a top surgeon at Vanderbilt who has restored Adam's ear from rib cartilage!

I believe the accident was the devil's attempt to stop our ministry before we ever opened the doors, but instead we were angry that he had attacked our son and more dedicated than ever to take the fight to him. Adam has been on his first mission trip and has been invited to speak at an upcoming city-wide crusade. In a little over the first year of our ministry, nearly 3,000 Christian comics have been distributed including a jail ministry and we are on our 3rd case of Bibles given out. Over 40 streets have had the gospel message shared. We have lots more on our hearts and will continue to be faithful as God opens the doors. Again, thank you for taking this time with me & God bless!

HOW TO CONTACT PASTOR CHRIS
Pastor Chris Shelton
Reach Out Christ's Kingdom (R.O.C.K.) Ministries
P.O. Box 111
Piggott, AR 72454
www.ReachOutChristsKingdom.org
Email: rock_ministries@live.com
We're also on facebook (R.O.C.K. Ministries) -
(Easiest for Pastor Chris to respond).

CPSIA information can be obtained at www.ICGtesting.com
Printed in the USA
LVOW13s1140010614

388005LV00001B/68/P